COMMUNITY · CONNECTIONS

?

Alex's
Lemonade
Stand

FOUNDATION FOR
CHILDHOOD CANCER ™

# ALEX'S LEMONADE STAND
## CHARITIES STARTED BY KIDS!
### BY MELISSA SHERMAN PEARL

CHERRY
LAKE
Publishing

Published in the United States of America by Cherry Lake Publishing
Ann Arbor, Michigan
www.cherrylakepublishing.com

Reading Adviser: Marla Conn MS, Ed., Literacy specialist, Read-Ability, Inc.

Photo Credits: © Photo used with permission from Alex's Lemonade Stand Foundation, cover, 5, 7, 11, 13, 15, 17, 19, 21; © Monkey Business Images/Shutterstock Images, 9

**LIBRARY OF CONGRESS CATALOGING-IN-PUBLICATION DATA HAS BEEN FILED AND IS AVAILABLE AT CATALOG.LOC.GOV**

Cherry Lake Publishing would like to acknowledge the work of The Partnership for 21st Century Learning. Please visit *www.p21.org* for more information.

Printed in the United States of America
Corporate Graphics

ALEX'S LEMONADE STAND

# CONTENTS

HOW DO THEY HELP?

# TAKING A STAND—AND MAKING ONE, TOO

More than 30 trillion **cells** make up the human body.  Cancer is a disease that gets in the way of healthy cells. Cancer cells can take over different parts of the body.  Though more common in older adults, sometimes **pediatric** cancers occur.  Alex's Lemonade Stand Foundation (ALSF) is a charity dedicated to helping kids fight this disease and win.

There are about 250,000 new childhood cancer patients every year worldwide.

As Alexandra "Alex" Scott neared her first birthday, she was diagnosed with neuroblastoma, a rare pediatric cancer. On January 19, 2000 (the day after her 4th birthday), Alex went into the hospital for a **stem cell transplant**. During her recovery, she announced that she wanted to hold a lemonade stand when she got home. But her parents, Liz and Jay, pointed out that winter weather might make for bad sales.

Lemonade stands have been popular in America for almost 150 years.

THINK!

In 2004, Alex's Lemonade Stand was moved from her front yard to her school, where it's still an annual fund-raiser. Do you have any annual community events in your neighborhood? Who do they help?

7

After she left the hospital, she kept asking about the lemonade stand. First it was once a month. Then it was once a week. Then it was every day. Her parents wondered why she wanted the money so badly. They said they'd be happy to buy her a new toy. But Alex didn't want anything for herself. She wanted to give the money she'd earn to doctors so they could help other kids.

New cancer treatments have helped to improve patient care, but research to create new treatments is very expensive.

Alex's Lemonade Stand has a program called Travel for Care. Based on its name, how do you think this program helps families? If you guessed that it helps families who travel for their child's treatment to pay for flights, **lodging**, meals, and gas, then you're right!

9

# TURNING LEMONS INTO LEMONADE

That spring, she held her first lemonade stand in front of her Connecticut home. Not only did her family and friends buy lemonade, but thanks to a newspaper story, many other people did, too. Exhausted but happy, she made $2,000 selling lemonade that day!

In early spring of 2001, the family of five moved to Philadelphia, closer to

Newspaper stories can help bring awareness and donations to local causes.

ADE STAND

ALSF tells lemonade stand hosts to plan to sell one cup every minute the stand is open. If you were planning on holding an event for 1½ hours, how much lemonade would you need? That's right—90 cups! And maybe a little extra, in case you get thirsty.

11

the best treatment for Alex's disease. Alex started talking about a lemonade stand again. Alex's second stand was held on a cold, October day. She made just under $800.

The following year, as spring neared, Alex had one thing on her mind: another lemonade stand. When Alex said she wanted to do it in memory of a hospital friend, her parents couldn't say no.

The Scott family made a flyer for Alex's school. One school parent shared it with the *Philadelphia Inquirer*.

Today, groups all over the country can hold lemonade stands for Alex's Lemonade Stand Foundation.

That newspaper ran a full-page story—and $2,000 in donations appeared even before Alex opened for business. She raised about $12,000.

As 2003 started warming up, so did Alex's lemonade excitement. She was ready with thousands of cups and gallons of lemonade. Even that day's pouring rain didn't **thwart** her effort. People from all over the city were lining up to be a part of Alex's dream. Another $18,000 was raised for the hospital.

14

Alex's foundation has been featured on *The Oprah Winfrey Show* and *The Today Show*.

Alex's Lemonade Stand Foundation hosts a Student Leadership Academy. What do you think are some of the skills that make someone a good leader? Look online or at the library to research common traits of good leaders.

15

# THE LEMONADE GIRL

Then things got really interesting. Alex started receiving letters every day from all around the world. People had seen or heard or read about her story and wanted to help. Sometimes the letters were just addressed to: The Lemonade Girl, United States. But the post office found her mailbox.  Alex was still **enduring** many hospital visits and

Many people, especially those in the Middle East, enjoy their lemonade with mint leaves!

treatments, but she loved how inspired others were.

Alex's 2004 lemonade stand was her last but her family continued holding the stands in her name. Before Alex passed away, she saw donations hit $1 million! Jay and Liz formed Alex's Lemonade Stand Foundation (ALSF) the next year and have dedicated their lives to running it.

ALSF is Alex's legacy. A legacy is something important you leave behind.

Gather some friends and create your own Alex's Lemonade Stand with proceeds benefiting ALSF. See how much you can get done by working together.

Since then, ALSF has raised over $140 million to fight childhood cancer. It has funded more than 700 **accredited** research projects across North America in the hopes of finding a cure. ALSF also funds programs that help families dealing with pediatric cancer as well as programs to empower youth to take a stand.

ALSF began in 2005, five years after Alex's first lemonade stand.

People have been using lemonade stands as a way to raise money for years. Ask your parents if they've ever held a lemonade stand. Ask other friends and family, too.

21

# GLOSSARY

**accredited** (uh-KRED-ih-tid) officially recognized or authorized

**cells** (SELZ) the smallest structural units of the human body

**enduring** (en-DOOR-ing) putting up with something difficult or painful

**lodging** (LAHJ-ing) a place in which someone stays temporarily

**pediatric** (pee-dee-AT-rik) relating to children

**stem cell transplant** (STEM SEL TRANS-plant) a procedure that involves introducing special cells into the body of someone with cancer in the hopes that they will rebuild the immune system

**thwart** (THWORT) to prevent a plan from happening or having success

# FIND OUT MORE

## WEB SITES

*www.alexslemonade.org*
Find out more about Alex's Lemonade Stand Foundation, its programs, and, of course, Alex.

*balconygardenweb.com/how-to-grow-lemon-tree-in-pot-complete-growing-guide/*
Lemon trees don't have to be grown in a big backyard. Take a look and see how you can grow lemons in a pot.

*www.acco.org*
The American Childhood Cancer Organization is the largest national grassroots organization in the battle against childhood cancer.

*kidshealth.org/en/kids/cancer.html*
Get information about cancer that's free of "doctor-speak."

# INDEX

## ABOUT THE AUTHOR

Melissa Sherman
Pearl is a mother
of two girls who
understands and
appreciates that you
don't have to be
an adult to make a
difference.